WHAT HAPPENS TO YOUR FOOD?

Alastair Smith

Illustrated by Maria Wheatley

Designed by Maria Wheatley and Ruth Russell

Digital artwork by John Russell

Series editor: Judy Tatchell

Your food's journey

After you swallow your food, it goes down a long, wiggly tube inside you.

The food slides down the wiggly food tube. It is broken up into tiny pieces.

Your body uses the tiny pieces to keep you going.

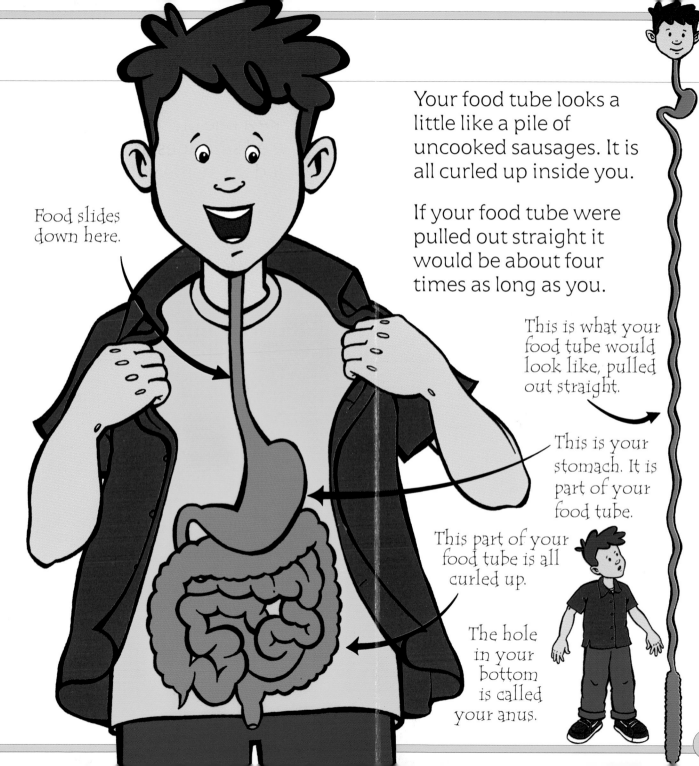

Food slides down here.

Your food tube looks a little like a pile of uncooked sausages. It is all curled up inside you.

If your food tube were pulled out straight it would be about four times as long as you.

This is what your food tube would look like, pulled out straight.

This is your stomach. It is part of your food tube.

This part of your food tube is all curled up.

The hole in your bottom is called your anus.

3

What shouldn't you eat?

You shouldn't eat things that have gone bad. Food goes bad when it gets old.

Also, beware of germs in food.

What are germs?

Germs are tiny creatures. They are too small for you to see. Some germs can make you ill if you eat them.

Making germs really hot is a good way to kill them. That's why you should cook meat and fish.

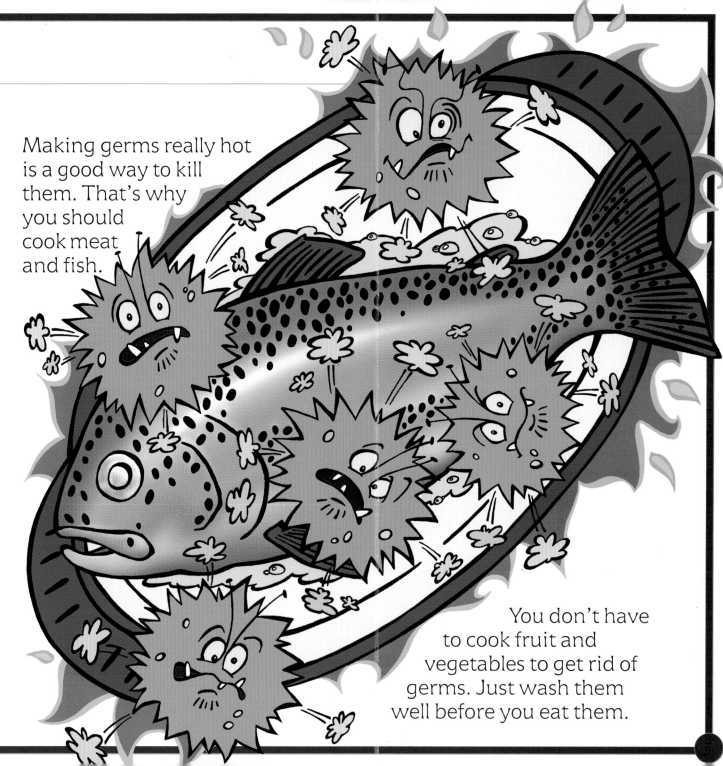

You don't have to cook fruit and vegetables to get rid of germs. Just wash them well before you eat them.

How can you get rid of germs?

Be a germ killer...

We love to live in meat and fish.

Please don't lift the flap!

Is it yummy?

How do you decide what you want to eat?

Look at it...

You decide whether you like the look of it.

Yuck!

Yum!

Smell it...

You decide whether you like the way it smells.

Remember it...

You remember what you thought of it last time you tasted it.

Taste it...

You decide whether you like the way it tastes.

Taste test

How do you taste different things?

What happens in your mouth?

Your mouth is a food masher. It changes the things you eat into a slippery paste. This paste is easy to swallow.

Your teeth chop your food up into little pieces.

Your tongue pushes the food around inside your mouth.

Spit makes food soft and slippery. It slides down your throat.

About your teeth

You have different types of teeth. They do different jobs.

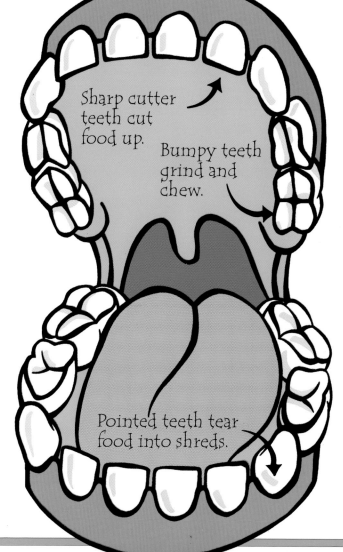

Sharp cutter teeth cut food up.

Bumpy teeth grind and chew.

Pointed teeth tear food into shreds.

Making food yummy

You can mix things together and cook them to make great new tastes.

Even making food look nice can help you to enjoy it.

Sauces or dressings can make things taste more interesting.

Different parts of your tongue taste different things.

sour

salty

bitter

sour

salty

sweet

Your tongue can taste sweet things, salty things, sour things and bitter things.

Sweet things taste sweetest on the tip of your tongue.

How many teeth?

Newborn babies have no teeth. You grow your first teeth when you are a few months old. You grow 20 baby teeth.

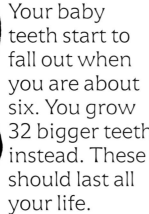

Your baby teeth start to fall out when you are about six. You grow 32 bigger teeth instead. These should last all your life.

Taking a bite

First you open wide, then ...

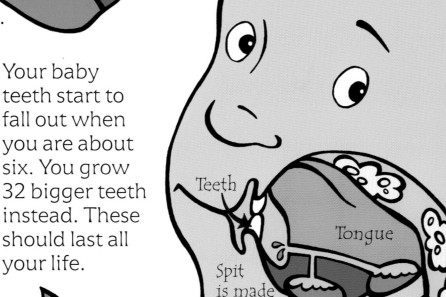

Teeth

Spit is made here.

Tongue

Windpipe

...Crunch! Chew! Chop!

Ball of food

Swallowing

Your tongue rolls chewed food into a ball. It pushes the ball to the back of your mouth.

You swallow and the food goes down your food tube.

Why do you choke?

Air goes down your windpipe when you breathe. Sometimes, food goes down the wrong way, into your windpipe. You choke to get the food out.

This ball of food is starting its journey through the food tube.

Into your stomach

Your food's next stop on its way down the food tube is in your stomach. This is like a squashy bag.

Where is your stomach?

Your stomach is about level with your elbows.

What does your stomach do?

Your stomach squeezes and mashes food up. It pours special stomach juices on the food. These help mush it up. It ends up like a slushy soup.

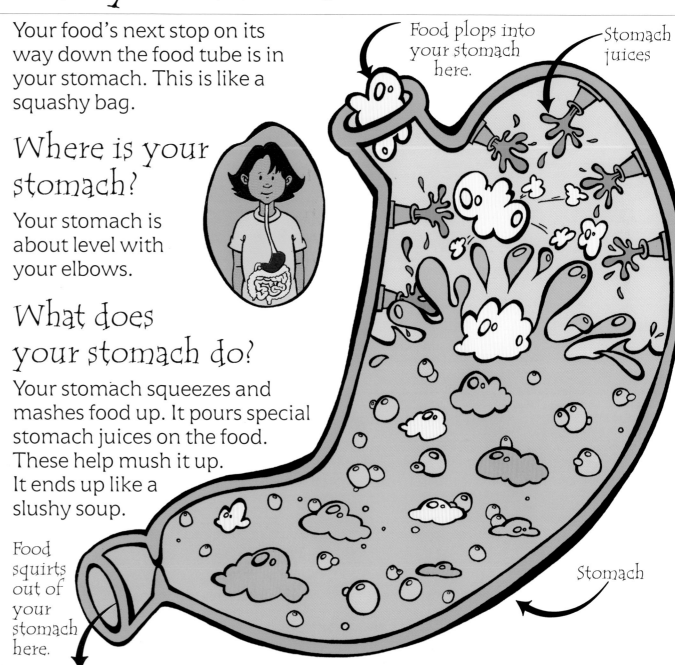

Food plops into your stomach here.

Stomach juices

Food squirts out of your stomach here.

Stomach

How big is your stomach?

If your stomach is empty it is about as big as this picture of a balloon. But your stomach can stretch to hold a big meal.

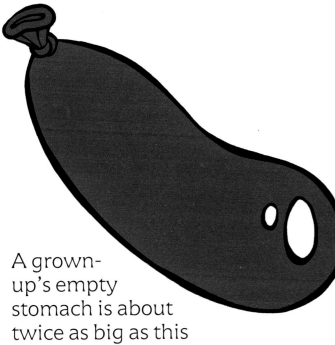

A grown-up's empty stomach is about twice as big as this picture of a balloon.

Eating too much

Sometimes you eat and drink too much. Your stomach might decide that it's had enough.

squeeze

zoom

Your stomach says NO!

Your stomach squeezes hard. It sends the food back up your food tube. This makes you sick. This is also called throwing up.

A horrible taste

Food that comes back up tastes horrible because it has lots of stomach juices in it. Stomach juices taste sour.

Eating bad food

Eating food that has gone bad can make you sick. It's your stomach's job to get rid of bad food before it harms you.

11

What happens next?

Where food goes next

The slushy food gets out of your stomach through a small hole. It squirts through the hole little by little.

Now it goes into a long, curled-up part of the food tube. This is your small intestine.

Moving along

The food tube squeezes food along all the way from your mouth to your anus.

It works like toothpaste being squeezed up a tube.

What's that noise?

After a meal you may hear gurgling noises coming from inside you. What's going on?

Don't worry, it's only your food being mashed and squeezed in your food tube.

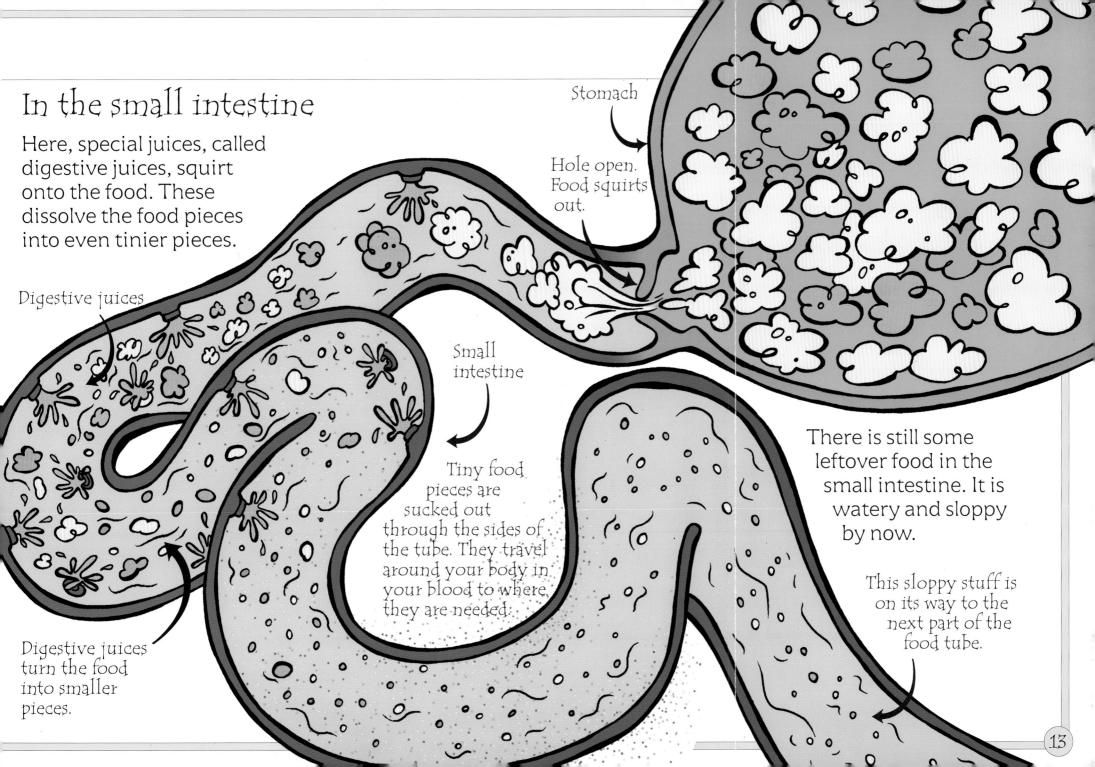

In the small intestine

Here, special juices, called digestive juices, squirt onto the food. These dissolve the food pieces into even tinier pieces.

Digestive juices

Digestive juices turn the food into smaller pieces.

Stomach

Hole open. Food squirts out.

Small intestine

Tiny food pieces are sucked out through the sides of the tube. They travel around your body in your blood to where they are needed.

There is still some leftover food in the small intestine. It is watery and sloppy by now.

This sloppy stuff is on its way to the next part of the food tube.

13

Stomach

The hole opens and closes to let food through. Here it is closed.

Where do the food pieces go next?

Let's get out of here!

Journey's end

At the end of your small intestine, food is squeezed into the next part of the food tube. This is called the large intestine.

The large intestine is wider and shorter than the small intestine.

The large intestine ends at your anus.

What happens here?

The large intestine works like a sieve. It sucks water out of the sloppy food through its sides.

The food left behind gets more solid and sludgy as water drains out.

Sloppy food

Water comes out through the sides.

What's in the sludgy stuff?

The sludgy stuff is mostly food your body cannot use.

There's still a little water left in the sludgy stuff. This helps it to slip and slide along.

This food isn't sloppy any more. It is soft and sludgy.

What happens then?

Let's go to the bathroom...

Bathroom

Index

First published in 1997 by Usborne Publishing Ltd, 83-85 Saffron Hill, London EC1N 8RT, England.

Printed in Italy

First published in America August 1997   UE